For Bill ~ *C.P.*
For Gesine ~ *N.M.*

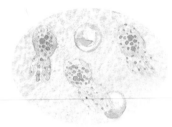

First American edition published 2003 by

CROCODILE BOOKS
An imprint of Interlink Publishing Group, Inc.
99 Seventh Avenue, Brooklyn, NY 11215 and
46 Crosby Street, Northtampton, Massachusets 01060
www.interlinkbooks.com

The publishers would like to thank Dr Antony Jensen at the
School of Ocean and Earth Science, University of Southampton, for his help

Published simultaneously in Great Britain in 2003 by Frances Lincoln Limited

Library of Congress Cataloging-in-Publication Data

Pitcher, Caroline.
Nico's octopus / Caroline Pitcher; illustrated by Nilesh Mistry.
p. cm.
Summary: Nico rescues a small octopus and takes it home to keep as a pet, caring for it until one day,
he learns some sad and wonderful news. Includes a factual section on octopuses.
ISBN 1-56656-483-2
[1. Octopus--Fiction.] I. Mistry, Nilesh, ill. II. Title.
PZ7.P6427 Ni 2003   [E]--dc21   2002012434

Printed in Singapore
1 3 5 7 9 8 6 4 2

Nico's Octopus

Caroline Pitcher

Illustrated by Nilesh Mistry

Crocodile Books, USA

An imprint of Interlink Publishing Group, Inc.
New York • Northampton

Nico set down his bucket of special stones
and watched the fishermen pull up their nets.
They were full to their brims with fish.
A shooting star had landed in one of them.
It had rays of pink light streaming out behind it.
"They've caught an alien!" cried Nico.
"No, it's not an alien," said a voice. "Not quite."

Nico turned around. An old fisherman sat under a lemon tree. His eyes were gray as sea mist.

"It's an octopus," he said. "You're lucky to find it."

"I've never seen a live one before," cried Nico. "I'm going to rescue it!"

Nico filled his bucket with sea water. Then he knelt down and gently picked up the octopus. It was as small as his fist.

He plopped it into the bucket and hurried past the fishermen's cafe. Octopuses of all sizes were hanging up to dry, like old gray bagpipes, waiting to be stewed with wine in a pot.

"Keep quiet, Octopus, or you'll be cooked too," whispered Nico.

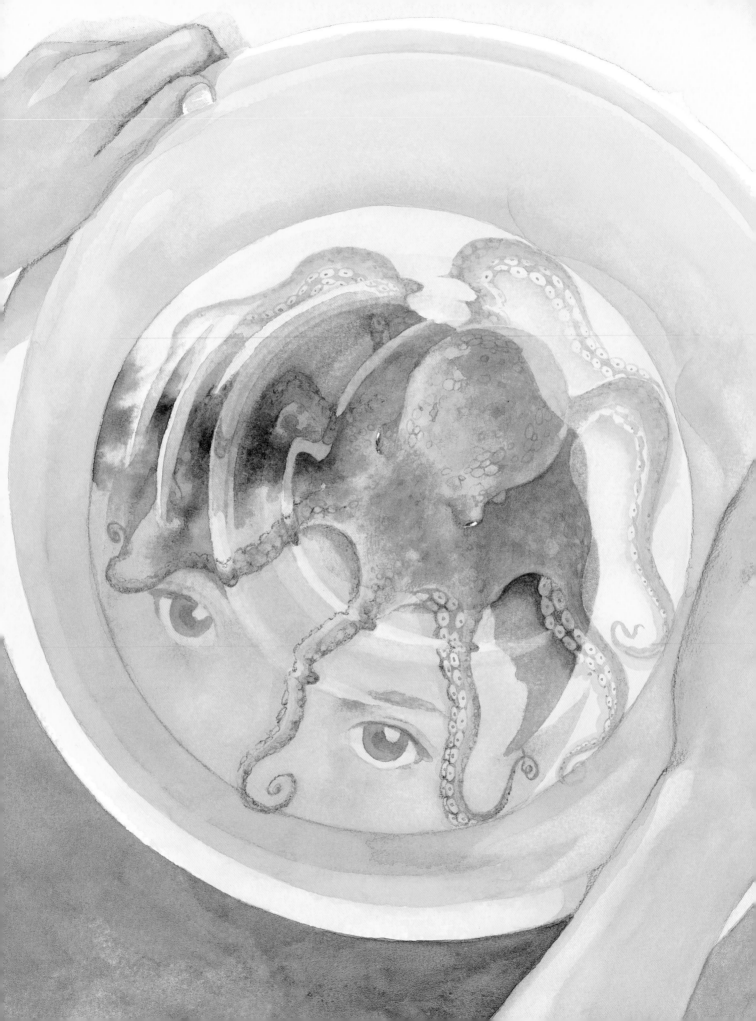

Nico hurried home and up to his bedroom. He peered nervously into the bucket.

The octopus had swelled as round as a spacecraft. It puffed out a little cloud of ink!

"You don't frighten me," said Nico. "Not as much as I frighten you. Now you've wrapped your legs all around yourself."

He touched the water. "Don't worry, Octopus. I'll take good care of you."

Suddenly the door burst open.

"What is that?" cried his mother.

"You can't keep that in here," cried his father.

"Please," begged Nico. "It's only a little octopus. Look!"

He pointed into the bucket – but the octopus wasn't there!

Nico searched under his bed and in his box of Legos.
At last he saw a curl of spaghetti waving at him from
an empty can.

"Ah! You can escape from anywhere, because you
haven't any bones!" he said.

"Then you had better get your octopus a tank with
a lid, Nico," smiled his mother.

Nico put his special stones and shells in the new tank.

The octopus crept off on tentacle-tip and hid every time it saw him. It could change color. It turned smooth pink near a rose-pink stone, mottled brown near a brown rock.

"You're the chameleon of the seas," said Nico. "I'm glad I rescued you."

Soon the octopus got to know him and sometimes, when it saw his face through the glass, it would reach out gently with the tip of its tentacle.

Nico caught crabs and small fish for the octopus. It hid behind a stone to eat its food. Bits of shell came out of its little tube, like a garbage chute out of a kitchen.

It was so clever! Nico put a little fish inside a bottle, and the octopus pulled out the cork to get it.

Nico hoped it did not miss the sounds of the sea. But he was sure it wasn't lonely. "I know you live on your own in the sea," he said. "Octopuses don't have families."

The sun beat down. Nico's room grew very hot.
When he opened his window, he heard the clash
of knives and forks from the café, and he whispered,
"I'm glad I got you before they did."

"It's a funny kind of pet," said his father. "It looks
as if it's from another planet. Why can't you just
have a cat or a goldfish?"

"Because I love my octopus," said Nico.

Then the worst thing in the world happened.
The octopus hid itself away. It would not eat.
It flushed red with anger and waved its tentacles
at Nico. Finally it collapsed like a broken umbrella.

Nico wrapped his arms around himself and cried.

"What's the matter, Nico?" said a voice. It was
the old fisherman.

"My octopus is ill," sobbed Nico, "and I don't
know why."

"May I see it?" said the fisherman.

Upstairs in Nico's room, the old fisherman gazed into the tank and said, "You are lucky, Nico. Your octopus has laid eggs."

"I thought it was a he, not a she," cried Nico.

"Look in her lair," said the fisherman. "It's hung with bead curtains. Those beads are eggs, thousands of them, as small as grains of rice."

"Your octopus is a good mother, Nico, and she really looks after her eggs. She even washes them. Thank goodness you rescued her from that net. Octopuses only lay eggs once in their lifetime, and then they die."

"You mean she will die now?" cried Nico.

"Yes. I'm sorry, Nico. She gives up her life for her babies."

Nico's octopus was growing weaker and weaker.

But the little octopuses sparked and burst out of their eggs. They shot up to the sunlight at the top of the tank, tiny rockets with tentacles streaming behind them. There they flickered like eight-legged fairy lights, red, pink, orange and purple.

Soon after that, Nico's octopus lay quite still.

Nico and the old fisherman waded into the sea with the baby octopuses.

The fisherman said, "When they are bigger, they will steal away and live alone, secretly, at the bottom of the sea."

Just like their mother, thought Nico. He had put her in a box lined with blue velvet. He placed it on the water and watched it spiral gently down into the sea.

"Goodbye, Octopus," he whispered.

Then he set her babies free, and the sea was spangled with little octopus stars.

About Octopuses

Octopuses belong to the same animal group as snails, squids, clams, and cuttlefish. This group has been in existence for hundreds of millions of years – the ancestors of modern octopuses lived at a time before fish evolved.

Octopuses vary in size from the giant North Pacific octopus, which can grow to about 11 yards (10 meters long) to the much smaller pygmy octopus, which reaches 4 inches (10 cm). The common octopus, which lives in warm waters around the world (in Europe from southern England southwards into the Mediterranean Sea and down the west African coast), reaches a length of nearly 4 feet (1.3 meters).

Octopuses generally live close to the coast in caves or crannies between rocks, although they can make burrows in sand. They feed on fish, clams, crabs, and prawns. They live for about 12–18 months, mating towards the end of their lives. The females die after tending their eggs, mostly because they do not feed during that time. The males do not live for long after they mate.

Octopuses are intelligent. They learn from experience and can remember what they have learned. Their brain development is the most complex of all animals without backbones and their suckers have an acute sense of touch. Their eyesight has evolved differently from that of land mammals: to focus, they move the lens in and out within the eye rather than changing the shape, as we do.

Octopuses use their ink to confuse predators and escape. They can release a cloud of ink to distract a crab or fish and then sneak around the back and grab it with their arms, using their suckers to hold on. They have a horned beak to bite and inject poison to kill their food quickly. One Australian species is so venomous that it can even kill a human being!

Octopuses are well known for their ability to change color and shape. They use color both for camouflage and to communicate their mood (they go white when they are afraid and red when they are angry).

Most remarkable of all, octopuses have three hearts to pump their blue blood around their body. No alien being from another galaxy could beat that!